# THE EIFFEL TOWER

By Christopher Ryan

PUBLISHED BY

## Capstone Press

Mankato, MN, U.S.A.

**Distributed By**

CHILDRENS PRESS®
CHICAGO

# CIP

## LIBRARY OF CONGRESS CATALOGING IN
## PUBLICATION DATA

Ryan, Christopher, 1952-
The Eiffel Tower / by Christopher Ryan.
p. cm. --(Inside story)
Summary: A boy learns from a French guide about the Eiffel Tower, its history and its builder.
**ISBN 1-56065-026-5**
1.Tour Eiffel (Paris, France)--Juvenile literature. [1. Eiffel Tower (Paris, France)] I. Title. II. Series: Inside story
(Mankato, Minn.)
NA2930.R93 1991
725'.97'0944361--dc2     **91-4286 CIP AC**

## PHOTO CREDITS

Art Resource: 4
French Government Tourist Office: 9, 15, 22, 27, 35, 36-37, 40


Designed by Nathan Y. Jarvis & Associates, Inc.

## Capstone Press

Box 669, Mankato, MN, 56001

# CONTENTS

# FRANCIS MEETS COLLETTE

Francis stood on the second platform of the Eiffel Tower. Far below him the River Seine glided through the city of Paris which spread away from the river's banks for miles. Broad boulevards full of traffic and colorful gardens seemed to sparkle in the sunlight.

Francis had been in France for two days with his parents. His parents stood a little way off, talking to another American couple they'd just met. A girl who looked to be a few years older than Francis was with the other couple. It looked as if they were having a good time and would be a while. Francis didn't mind waiting. It was fun watching the tiny people and cars way down on the ground below. He leaned against a railing and listened to the wind moan softly through the tower.

A voice behind him shook Francis out of his day-dream. Startled, he turned and saw the girl. She had joined him at the railing.

"Hi, there," the girl said. "You can see a very long way from up here, can't you?"

Francis noticed she had just a little accent. It sounded French. But she seemed to speak American very well.

"Hello," said Francis. "Yes, you can see very far. And everything down there looks so small."

"Do you mind if I talk to you?" the girl asked.

"No," said Francis. "I think my parents are going to be busy for a while. Are those people your parents? You sound a little like you might be from France."

"I am from France originally. But those aren't my parents. I spent eight years in America, and now I take people on tours of the tower. I just finished a tour, and those people had some questions."

"I like your accent," Francis said. "What would you like to talk about?"

"Well, how much do you know about this tower?"

"Only that it's always been the first thing I think about when somebody talks about Paris."

"I'm not surprised," the girl said. "The Eiffel Tower is famous all over the world. Tell me your name, and I'll tell you about the tower. It has always been my favorite place in France. I've read everything I could find about it, and I once wrote an essay on it for a history class."

"My name's Francis."

"Pleased to meet you, Francis. My name is Collette."

# HARD TIMES GIVE WAY TO GOOD TIMES

Collette leaned against the railing and started her story.

You can't really understand the Eiffel Tower until you know a little about France before the tower was built, she told Francis. In the French Revolution in 1789, the French people changed the kind of government they had. Before, they were ruled by kings and queens. That kind of government was called a **monarchy**. Their new government was supposed to be like America's, a **democracy**. But for almost a hundred years, France couldn't seem to form a government that could last. There were wars and revolutions and the French people often suffered terribly.

Finally, in 1870, the French fought the Germans in what was called the Franco-Prussian War. France's army was defeated in just a few weeks. The Germans surrounded Paris and cut off all the food supplies. People were forced to eat rats, cats and zoo animals.

Germany captured two French provinces

France, Paris and the location of the Eiffel Tower.

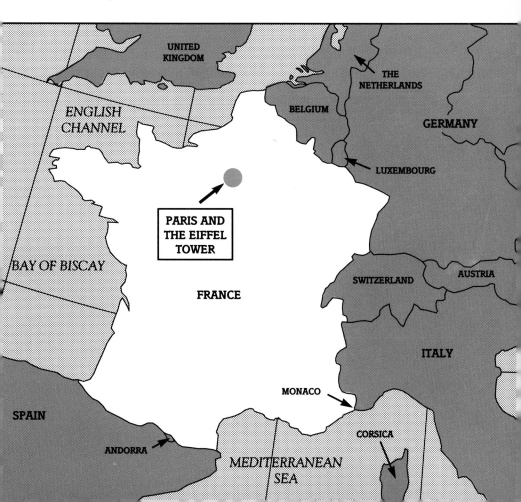

called Alsace and Lorraine. A million and a half French people lived in Alsace and Lorraine. The French also lost mines and important industries in the two provinces.

Then, early in the 1870s, things started to get better. The French government decided to make the country a **republic** instead of a monarchy. In only a few decades, France's people were much better off, and the country caught up with other nations in business and industry.

Many people say that the early 1870s were the beginning of the good times, what the French call the **Belle Epoque**. The Eiffel Tower was an important part of those times. In fact, for a lot of people it came to stand for everything good that happened.

# A BIG IDEA AND SOME STRANGE IDEAS

Collette stopped talking and looked out over the city. She seemed lost in thought.

"What did all those problems have to do with the Eiffel Tower?" Francis asked.

"Well, you see," Collette answered, "France had become a republic. It was finally what it had started out wanting to be in 1789. The government wanted to celebrate. The hundredth anniversary of the Revolution was just a few years off. France's prime minister at the time, Jules Ferry, decided to hold a world's fair."

"You mean like the world's fairs we have now?"

"Yes. He wanted to show the world how

France had become a leader in business, industry and engineering. It turned out to be the most successful world's fair up to that time. Thirty-two million people attended."

"I still don't understand what all this has to do with the Eiffel Tower," Francis said.

"My, but you're impatient," Collette answered. "You should know that huge monuments like the Eiffel Tower don't just happen. There's always a lot of history behind them. And you won't understand the monument if you don't know something about the people and country where it was built."

Francis felt a little embarrassed. "I'm sorry, Collette," he said. "I just don't know how much longer I can stay here. My mom and dad might want to leave." He looked around at his parents. They were still talking with the other Americans.

"That's all right," said Collette, and she smiled warmly. "Don't worry. They look like they could be here all day. Anyway, we're almost to the good part."

Collette told Francis that after the prime minister suggested a world's fair, a man named Edouard Lockroy had another idea. Lockroy was France's minister of commerce and industry. He wanted someone to build a one thousand-foot tower. Such a tall tower, reaching to the sky, would be a symbol of progress.

"Of course, it wasn't only Edouard Lockroy's idea," Collette went on. "Lots of engineers had been thinking about a thousand-foot tower for years."

She told Francis about Richard Trevithick who wanted to build one in London in 1833. And there were two Americans who would have put one up in Philadelphia to help celebrate America's one-hundredth birthday in 1876. The people in charge of the Philadelphia Centennial Exposition said it would look like a factory chimney. They wouldn't let the two men build it. The tallest tower before the Eiffel Tower was the Washington Monument in America. It was 555 feet high.

"That's only about half as tall as the Eiffel Tower," said Francis.

"You might not be very patient," Collette said. "But you're pretty smart."

Collette told Francis that the government in Paris was very slow about finding someone to build the thousand-foot tower. By the time they announced a contest for the best designs, **architects** and **engineers** only had 16 days to draw the plans. Still, there were more than 100 entries.

"Some of the ideas people had for the tower were really funny," Collette said. "Some were even scary." She went on to tell about one plan for a huge lawn sprinkler that would water Paris during droughts. Another was for a giant guillotine. That was the machine used to cut off people's heads during the French Revolution. One man wanted to set up lights and mirrors on his tower. He said Paris would never have night again. Anywhere in the city at night you would get eight times more light than you needed to read a newspaper.

"None of those ideas won the contest," Collette said. "The man who won was Alexandre Gustave Eiffel. I like to call him Gusty for short. He worried about wind all the time. But I'll tell you about that later.

"As it turned out, Gusty had a head start. He was 53 at the time and was already known as France's master builder in metal. The chief of research for his company, Maurice Koechlin, had already designed the tower in 1884. The committee in charge of the contest had seen the plan and had it in mind when they wrote down the rules for the design contest. They thought Eiffel's tower was

14

practical. And almost anything was more practical than the giant lawn sprinkler, don't you think?"

Francis didn't answer. He just smiled and listened.

Collette said that Eiffel wanted to build with metal because the tower was too tall to be built with stone. Large buildings like cathedrals had all been built with stone until that time. But Eiffel believed there would be

**Gusty designed the tower using wrought iron and rivets to keep it strong in the high winds.**

too much weight on the **foundation**. The pressure of one stone pressing against another to a height of 1,000 feet would destroy the **mortar** that held them together. The whole thing would finally fall down.

Three kinds of metal were used in Eiffel's day. He looked at each one. **Cast iron** was too brittle. **Steel** was too flexible, and it cost too much. Eiffel chose **wrought iron**. It was strong, but it didn't weigh too much. The tower could be taken down after the world's fair if that's what the government wanted to do.

"Gusty had been building bridges and other things out of metal for 30 years," Collette said. "He knew what he was doing. And that was a good thing. He had only two years to build the tallest tower on earth. The Washington Monument took 36 years to build."

# BUILDING THE TOWER

"On January 26, 1887," Collette said, "workers started digging the foundation for the Eiffel Tower."

"At last," said Francis.

"Now, now," Collette said.

"I'm sorry. Go on."

"All right. Well, even though he didn't have much time, Gusty was careful. Nobody had ever done anything like his project before. He had the people who drew the plans for the tower draw plans for every piece of metal. That meant drawing 18,038 pieces. It took 30 people 18 months to do the job."

"Why was he so careful?"

"Most of the pieces of the tower are held together by **rivets**. A rivet is like a metal bolt with a head on one end. The pieces of metal that have to be held together have holes in them. Workers line up the holes and put a very hot rivet through them. Then, because the rivet is soft from being so hot, someone can hit it hard with a hammer on the end that doesn't have a head and make it into a two-headed bolt. So the pieces of metal are held together.

"The important thing is that those holes in the pieces of metal had to line up every time as the tower was put together. Otherwise, somebody would have to start making some holes larger or even making new holes. And there'd be no end to that. Gusty just didn't have time for mistakes. He decided everything had to be exact to one-tenth of a millimeter. That's about one-sixteenth of an inch."

"He reminds me of my math teacher," said Francis. "She won't let us get away with even a little, tiny mistake."

"In engineering, little mistakes can become big ones," Collette said. "Gusty knew that. For example, when he designed the foundation, he put in **jacks** that could lift and lower the four corners of the tower. Each of those jacks could lift 900 tons. When the four curved corner pieces of the tower were joined together at the first platform, Eiffel could be sure the rest of the tower would be perfectly vertical. He didn't want to end up with a leaning tower."

"If those jacks had to lift 900 tons," Francis said, "the tower must be very heavy."

"It isn't really," Collette said. "Let's say you built a tube that was the same size around as the base of the Eiffel tower and the same height. Then let's say you stood that tube next to the tower. You'd find that just the air inside the tube weighed 2,000 tons more than the tower."

"Still, it must be pretty heavy."

"About 10,600 tons. It won't blow away. But like I said before, Gusty was worried about wind anyway."

"Why?" Francis asked.

"A lot of people who called themselves engineers in those days did their planning by guessing what was best. Sometimes they didn't think about things like wind. They'd build a huge railroad bridge without thinking about what the wind might do to it when a train was rolling across. And pretty soon there'd be a bad accident. It happened more than once."

Gustave Eiffel was a careful man and a very good mathematician, Collette told Francis. None of the bridges he built fell down. Some are still used today.

Wind was Eiffel's special worry. When he built the tower, he figured out what would happen if the wind reached 148 miles per hour. That was higher than any wind ever recorded in Paris. He knew the tower would stand.

"The odd thing," Collette said, "is that the tower stands up against the wind so well because a lot of it isn't there."

"What?" asked Francis, startled.

"Look at it. It's full of holes. The pieces of metal aren't solid. You can hear the wind whistling right on through. It doesn't have anything to push against. The tower is a lot lighter than it would have been if it were solid. If it were solid and weighed as little as it does, it might blow over."

Francis looked a little nervous. "Blow over?" he said, looking down to the ground below him.

"Relax," Collette said. "It's still here a hundred years after it was finished."

Francis felt better. "There's something I don't understand," he said. "How did the workers get these big pieces of iron from the ground all the way to the top of the tower?"

"That was a real problem," Collette said. "Eiffel didn't have the big construction **cranes** we use to build our skyscrapers today. He had to find another way."

"What did he do?"

"He used creeping cranes."

"That's a funny name. How did they work?"

Collette explained that creeping cranes worked a little like a railroad. When railroads were built, workers laid the track in front of their supply trains. The supply train just followed along as tracks were laid to carry it. Creeping cranes followed along as workers built tracks for the tower's elevator system. As the tower grew, the cranes just moved higher.

"So that's how the Eiffel tower was built," said Collette. "It was the tallest structure in the world until 1929, when the Chrysler Building was finished in New York. You can see that it has three platforms. Here on the second platform you're about 380 feet above the ground."

"And at the very top it's a thousand feet high," Francis said.

"Well," said Collette, "not quite. It's about 986 feet. But that's close enough. And the nine-hundred-eighty-six-foot tower doesn't sound as good as the thousand-foot tower. Anyway, with the television tower on top, it's really more than a thousand feet tall."

"Was the tower finished on time?" Francis asked.

"The tower was," Collette answered. "But the elevators weren't working until about a month after the fair opened. That wasn't Eiffel's fault, though. He didn't have control of building the elevators."

"Mr. Eiffel must have been very smart," said Francis.

"Yes, he was. But here comes somebody who looks like she wants to talk to you."

Francis looked around. "It's my mom," he whispered. "If I can stay longer, will you tell me more about Mr. Eiffel?"

"Sure."

Francis's mother walked up to him and said, "Honey, would you mind if we stayed and talked to our new friends for a while longer? I don't want you to get bored."

"Bored?" Francis laughed. "It's hard to get bored up here." He told his mom not to worry. She went back to talk with Francis's dad and their friends.

"Let's talk about Gustave Eiffel," said Collette.

# THE TOWER
# BUILDER

This is the story Collette told Francis about the life of Gustave Eiffel.

The man who would build the Eiffel Tower was born December 15, 1832. His name then was Alexandre Gustave Boenickhausen-Eiffel. He shortened it to Alexandre Gustave Eiffel in 1880.

As a boy, Eiffel was only a fair student. But when he was a little older, two of his teachers got him interested in history and literature. He began to do very well in school. Finally, he was sent to a special school that prepared students to enter the most famous college in France, the Ecole Polytechnique. But Eiffel failed an important exam and had to go to another college. He wasn't upset. The other school was very good, too.

At the Ecole Centrale des Arts et Manufactures, Gustave studied chemical engineering. He wanted to work for his uncle who made vinegar. Chemical engineering would help him in his career. When Eiffel graduated, he knew very little about building with metal.

Before Eiffel could start work in his uncle's vinegar distillery, his uncle and his parents argued about politics and didn't get along anymore. Eiffel had to find another job. He started working for a company that built railroad equipment. He was soon made chief of research.

Eiffel's first big project was a 1,600-foot bridge across the Garonne River at Bordeaux, France. While working on the bridge, he showed he wasn't afraid to use new methods. He also became a hero when he saved a worker who fell into the river while working on the bridge. When the job was done, in 1860, the workers gave him a medal.

Eiffel married Marie Gaudelet in 1862. They had five children. Marie died 15 years later, and Eiffel never remarried.

In 1864, Eiffel started his own metal

construction business near Paris. He went to work to find ways to make construction more scientific and safer. He wanted to know exactly what stress and strain did to pieces of iron in bridges and buildings.

Eiffel and Company built iron arches for a building at the Paris Universal Exposition in 1867. They were the largest arches ever built. Then the company built the highest bridge in the world, completing it in 1884. Because Eiffel knew exactly how iron works, he could build huge structures both quickly and safely.

One of Gustave's most famous projects was the Statue of Liberty that now stands in New York Harbor. The statue was meant to show friendship between France and America. A French artist designed the statue, but he didn't know how to build it. It had to be very large. It also had to be sent across the Atlantic ocean in pieces. It would be put together in America.

Eiffel had the answer to the artist's problem. He made a light, iron framework to hold the statue up. That way, the statue could be hollow instead of solid. The iron framework, covered with copper, could be loaded on a ship in pieces and sent across the ocean.

Eiffel went on putting up bridges and buildings in Europe and in South America. When he finished the Eiffel Tower in 1889, he started working on the Panama Canal to design and build the huge **locks** that allow ships to pass between the Atlantic Ocean and the Pacific. But a scandal ended France's part in the work on the canal. Because of the scandal, Eiffel's reputation as a builder was badly hurt. He wasn't to blame, but people no longer hired him to build.

Eiffel was a man who didn't give up. He couldn't go on building bridges and towers, so he found other things to do. He turned the tower into a kind of laboratory where he and other people could do experiments. For the first time, France's Central Weather Bureau could measure temperatures and wind speeds at 1,000 feet and at ground level directly below. Eiffel also built a new kind of shelter for thermometers and other weather instruments. And he even designed better instruments. From 1903 to 1912, he published facts about the weather and helped make meteorology a respected science in France.

Around 1900, Gustave became interested in flight. He set up experiments to study how air flowing around an airplane wing helps it stay up. At the foot of the Eiffel Tower, he built the best **wind tunnel** in the world. The tunnel let him control how fast the wind blew as he tested his airplane models. He discovered that air flowing over the wing lifts an airplane better than air striking the wing underneath, a fundamental principle of aerodynamics. He also made great progress in designing propellers.

Finally, though, the wind tunnel had to be shut down. It made too much noise and bothered the neighbors.

For his work on flight, Eiffel was given the Langley Gold Medal in 1913. It was the same medal the famous Wright Brothers had been given in 1910. The man who presented the medal to Eiffel was Alexander Graham Bell who invented the telephone.

At the end of his life, Eiffel was happy that his tower had so many practical uses. But he'd always thought it also was beautiful. He believed it should stand even if it had no "practical" use. Today, many people agree with him.

Alexandre Gustave Eiffel died on December 27, 1923. He was 91 years old.

# THE TOWER IN WAR AND PEACE

"Were there any other ways the tower was useful besides for science?" Francis asked.

"Oh, yes," Collette answered. "You might say the Eiffel Tower brought radio and television to France.

"It started in 1898. Eiffel invited a man to start transmitting radio signals from the third platform. Ten years later, signals from the tower reached as far as North America. During World War One, the tower had a permanent station. It picked up signals from the German army that helped the French and their allies win the war. After World War One, that station was turned over to civilians, and it began playing news and music.

"In 1925, the tower was used for early experiments in television. The first French TV station began operating here in 1953."

"What other things has the tower been used for," Francis asked.

"Let's see," said Collette, thinking. "It was used as a giant advertising billboard in 1925. The advertiser used 250,000 lights in six colors and 375 miles of wiring to sell cars. In 1933, the tower was turned into a huge clock. It was the world's largest with a face 50 feet across. Then a thermometer was added in 1934. The degree marks were eight feet apart. And in 1937, there was another world's fair in Paris. Six miles of fluorescent tubes outlined the tower then."

Collette paused for a breath. "Oh, I almost forgot," she said. "The first person to fly an airplane across the Atlantic used the tower. For Charles Lindbergh, it was a landmark that helped him find a place to land."

"What about World War Two?" asked Francis. "Did anything happen at the tower then?"

"The Eiffel Tower was very important during World War Two," Collette said. "It was a symbol of freedom for the French. I think the story of Lucien Sarniquet, who was a captain in the Paris fire department, will tell you what I mean."

Collette straightened, and her eyes

sparkled. "It is something that makes me proud to know I was born French," she said. It took her quite a while to tell the story because she wanted to include all the details. Here's a shorter version.

During World War Two, the Germans captured Paris in 1940. Lucien Sarniquet had to take the flag down from the Eiffel Tower when the German army took over. He promised himself he would be the first to raise the French flag again when the Germans were gone.

Lucien watched and waited. The war turned against the Germans. By August of 1944, the French struggle against the Germans was at a turning point. Soldiers were fighting in the streets of Paris. Lucien knew that his people needed something to help keep their morale high if they were to win. He decided August 25 was the day to raise the French flag on the Eiffel Tower again.

At noon, Lucien arrived at the base of the tower. He was joined by two other men. Together they started climbing the 1,671 steps to the top. With them they carried a flag Lucien had made from old bed sheets.

Suddenly, bullets began bouncing off the iron around them. Some German soldiers had seen them and opened fire. Lucien and his friends kept climbing.

In fact, Lucien wasn't as worried about the bullets as about something else. He had spotted two other people above him on the steps. They had a flag, too. He tried to get to the top first, but he was too far behind. The flag went up, but it wasn't Lucien's.

In the end, though, the fire department captain didn't mind. The occupation of Paris by the Germans was over. He hugged the people who had beaten him to the top of France's symbol of freedom.

"That's a fine story," Francis said.

"It is a good one," said Collette. "It shows how much the French people had come to love their tower. The Germans knew how important the tower was, too. In 1942, they said they would tear it down and cut it up for scrap metal. But they were worried the French would become so angry they'd revolt. So they changed their minds."

"I'm glad they did," Francis said. "The tower means so much to so many people."

# SOME UNHAPPY VOICES

Collette turned away from Francis and looked out over the city. Then she seemed to sigh, and she turned back to face him.

"Not everybody has been happy with the tower," she said. "When it was being built, there were quite a few people who complained."

"What did they say?" Francis asked.

"A lot of people were afraid the tower would fall down. After all, nothing that tall had ever been built. Once, some people who lived nearby went to court and stopped construction on the tower for a while. They were worried it would fall and crush their house. A mathematics professor once claimed the tower would fall over when it reached exactly 748 feet.

"Other people had even stranger worries. At least they seem strange to us. A newspaper story in Paris said the tower was changing the weather around the city. The writer said the tower wouldn't let storms travel. All that metal was capturing all the electricity in the storms and wearing them out."

L'Arc de Triumph is another popular landmark in Paris.

A view of the Eiffel Tower at night from the Siene River.

"Did people believe those things?" Francis asked.

"Some people did." Collette answered. "But the worst attacks on the tower came from writers and artists who thought it would destroy the beauty of Paris."

"But it is beautiful. Why would artists and writers think it isn't?"

"Today the Eiffel Tower is important in paintings, books, poems and movies," Collette said. "But that's because it has had time to become part of Paris and part of the world. It's beautiful now because people know it means something. For one thing, it stands for freedom, just like the Statue of Liberty."

"What did some writers and artists say about the tower?" Francis asked.

"One writer, Guy de Maupassant, ate lunch in one of the restaurants in the tower. He said he ate there because it was the only place in Paris where he couldn't see the tower. He couldn't see it, of course, because he was inside it. Other people called it a 'skinny pyramid of iron ladders,' a 'disgraceful skeleton' and a 'tragic lamppost'."

"Those are terrible things to say. How did Mr. Eiffel take them?"

"Gusty knew what he was doing. He

thought his tower was beautiful. As a matter of fact, a lot of the people who complained about the tower at first learned to admire it later."

## SOME SILLINESS AND A FRIENDLY GOOD-BYE

"From a lot of what I've told you, you might think the Eiffel Tower is a very serious place," Collette said. "But the tower hasn't just been a site for scientific experiments and valiant acts during war."

"What do you mean?" asked Francis.

"You'd be surprised at some of the antics that have gone on here," Collette answered. "Back in 1891 a Paris baker climbed all the way to the first platform. That's 363 stairs. And he did it on stilts."

"That is pretty silly," Francis said. "What else happened?"

"In 1906, there was a foot race up the

41

tower. The winner made it to the first platform in only three minutes and 14 seconds. But the real standout was a fellow who made it to the second platform in eight minutes. He was carrying 100 pounds of cement."

Collette told Francis about all sorts of acrobatics and stunts that had taken place at the tower over the years. In 1923, someone rode a bicycle down the steps from the first platform. A man climbed the tower to the top on one leg in 1959. A cow named Kilkee was hauled up the tower to advertise dairy products in 1968. That same year a man carried his television up to the first platform and threw it off because he didn't like the programs.

One of the most outrageous proposals for the tower came in 1969. Someone suggested that an artificial ski slope be constructed from the first platform to the ground.

"So the tower has had quite a colorful history," said Collette. "It has been a place where people of all kinds have found something to enjoy and think about."

"I guess that makes it useful and beautiful," said Francis.

"You are smart." Collette said. "Now, I must go. Your parents are coming this way, and I have to start another tour. It has been fun talking with you."

"You sure know a lot about the Eiffel Tower, Collette," Francis said. Collette held out her hand, and Francis shook it. "I hope I'll see you again before I leave France."

"If you don't, look for me in America, Francis," Collette said, as she walked away to begin her next tour. "I'm planning a visit to the Statue of Liberty."

# GLOSSARY

**ARCHITECTS-** Professional who designs and draws plans for buildings and other structures.

**BELLE EPOQUE-** Time of good feelings in France before World War I.

**CAST IRON-** Hard, rather brittle metal. Breaks more easily than steel or wrought iron.

**CRANE-** Machine with a movable arm made to lift and carry heavy objects.

**DEMOCRACY-** Government ruled by the people to preserve equal rights and opportunities.

44

**ENGINEERS**- Someone trained in a branch of engineering, such as mechanical or chemical engineering. A professional in a branch of engineering.

**FOUNDATION**- The base, often beneath the ground's surface, on which a structure rests.

**JACKS**- Machine used to lift a heavy object.

**LOCK**- Part of a canal equipped with gates that let water in and out to raise or lower the water level and float ships from one level to another.

**MONARCHY**- Government headed by one person, such as a king or queen.

**MORTAR**- Cement, sand and water mixed together and used to hold bricks or stones together in a structure.

**REPUBLIC**- Government in which representatives are elected by the people to rule the country.

**RIVETS-** Metal bolt with a head on one end used to hold pieces of metal together. The bolt is heated, inserted through holes in the pieces of metal and struck on the end without a head. The blow forms a second head and secures the pieces of metal.

**STEEL-** Hard, flexible metal that resists rust.

**WIND TUNNEL-** Chamber for testing scale models of airplanes for the effects of wind. The speed of the wind can be controlled for accurate measurements.

**WROUGHT IRON-** Tough metal that resists corrosion and can be shaped into decorative forms.